# DO THE WORK!
# NO POVERTY

## COMMITTING TO THE UN'S SUSTAINABLE DEVELOPMENT GOALS

**JULIE KNUTSON**

CHERRY LAKE PRESS

Published in the United States of America by Cherry Lake Publishing Group
Ann Arbor, Michigan
www.cherrylakepublishing.com

Reading Adviser: Beth Walker Gambro, MS, Ed., Reading Consultant, Yorkville, IL
Photo Credits: © Jne Valokuvaus/Shutterstock.com, cover, 1; © Alexandros Michailidis/Shutterstock.com, 5;
Infographic From The Sustainable Development Goals Report 2020, by United Nations Department of Economic
and Social Affairs © 2020 United Nations. Reprinted with the permission of the United Nations, 7; © Nelson
Antoine/Shutterstock.com, 8; © Yury Birukov/Shutterstock.com, 10; © Kitja Kitja/Shutterstock.com, 13;
© addkm/Shutterstock.com, 14; © RossHelen/Shutterstock.com, 16; © Joa Souza/Shutterstock.com, 19;
© Moha El-Jaw/Shutterstock.com, 20; © Eak. Temwanich/Shutterstock.com, 23; © Syda Productions/
Shutterstock.com, 24; © Prostock-studio/Shutterstock.com, 27

**Cherry Lake Press** is an imprint of Cherry Lake Publishing Group.

Library of Congress Cataloging-in-Publication Data
Names: Knutson, Julie, author.
Title: Do the work! : no poverty / by Julie Knutson.
Description: Ann Arbor, Michigan : Cherry Lake Publishing, 2022. | Series: Committing to the
    UN's sustainable development goals | Audience: Grades 4-6
Identifiers: LCCN 2021036394 (print) | LCCN 2021036395 (ebook) | ISBN 9781534199231 (hardcover) |
    ISBN 9781668900376 (paperback) | ISBN 9781668906132 (ebook) | ISBN 9781668901816 (pdf)
Subjects: LCSH: Sustainable development—Juvenile literature. | Poverty—Prevention—Juvenile literature.
Classification: LCC HC79.E5 K588 2022 (print) | LCC HC79.E5 (ebook) | DDC 338.9/27—dc23
LC record available at https://lccn.loc.gov/2021036394
LC ebook record available at https://lccn.loc.gov/2021036395

Cherry Lake Publishing Group would like to acknowledge the work of the Partnership for 21st Century
Learning, a Network of Battelle for Kids. Please visit http://www.battelleforkids.org/networks/p21
for more information.

Printed in the United States of America
Corporate Graphics

The content of this publication has not been approved by the United Nations and does not reflect the views of the
United Nations or its officials or Member States. For more information on the Sustainable Development Goals please visit
https://www.un.org/sustainabledevelopment.

# ABOUT THE AUTHOR

Julie Knutson is an author-educator who writes extensively about global citizenship and the
Sustainable Development Goals. Her previous book, *Global Citizenship: Engage in the Politics
of a Changing World* (Nomad Press, 2020), introduces key concepts about 21st-century
interconnectedness to middle grade and high school readers. She hopes that this series will
inspire young readers to take action and embrace their roles as changemakers in the world.

# TABLE OF CONTENTS

# CHAPTER 1

# Meet the SDGs

Quick, close your eyes! Now . . . imagine a world where every person has food, clean water, and shelter. Imagine a world in which *every* child has access to books and quality education. In this world, all people can go to the doctor when they are sick. In this world, all people—regardless of race, religion, age, gender, ability, or social class—are treated equally.

This is the world that the people behind the **United Nations**' (UN) 17 **Sustainable** Development Goals (SDGs) want to create. They want to achieve it by 2030, and they need your help!

The flag of the United Nations features the official emblem of the UN.

## What Are the SDGs?

This set of goals "for people and the planet" provides a blueprint for a better world. All 191 UN member states have agreed to cooperate in reaching the 169 SDGs targets in the coming decade.

The first goal on the UN's list is a huge one—"No Poverty." Why is this goal, which aims to "end poverty in all its forms everywhere," first? What exactly is poverty, and how does it relate to the other goals on the list? What are some actions that we can take to tackle this global challenge?

Read on to explore and learn more!

# Defining Poverty

Extreme poverty happens when people don't have money for food, safe drinking water, shelter, and clothing. These basic needs are core human rights, meaning that each person on the planet deserves them. Making sure that everyone's human rights are respected and upheld is part of our responsibilities as global citizens.

According to the **World Bank**, the minimum amount of money that people need to live is $1.90 per person, per day. This is called the global poverty line. The World Bank determines this number by averaging the cost of bare essentials in the world's 15 poorest countries. People's needs vary by country and climate, and each country sets its own standards for what defines "basic needs." This means that a person's basic needs might differ in Iran, Ireland, or India.

Poverty exists both in cities and in rural areas. It affects people of all ages, from birth to death. Its causes are complicated and are rooted in deep histories, often beyond an individual's control. In some areas, cycles of poverty result from **colonial** systems of the past.

# END POVERTY IN ALL ITS FORMS EVERYWHERE

## THE WORLD
# WAS **OFF TRACK** TO END POVERTY BY **2030**

15.7%

10%

8.2%

6%

2010    2015    2019    2030

## YOUNG WORKERS ARE
## TWICE AS LIKELY TO BE
## LIVING IN EXTREME POVERTY
## AS ADULT WORKERS [2019]

COVID-19 IMPLICATIONS

## COVID-19 CAUSES
## THE FIRST INCREASE
IN GLOBAL POVERTY IN DECADES

**+71 MILLION** PEOPLE ARE PUSHED INTO **EXTREME POVERTY** IN **2020**

## 4 BILLION PEOPLE
DID NOT BENEFIT
FROM ANY FORM OF
SOCIAL PROTECTION IN 2016

## NATURAL DISASTERS
## EXACERBATE POVERTY

## $23.6 BILLION
DIRECT ECONOMIC LOSSES
[FROM 63 COUNTRIES IN 2018]

SUSTAINABLE DEVELOPMENT G❂ALS

People in line to receive food donations during COVID-19.

**STOP AND THINK:** *The UN estimates that more than 700 million people, about 10 percent of the world's population, live in extreme poverty today.*

Poverty can be caused or worsened by both small- and large-scale events. At the personal level, the absence or death of a family member can put a person or family at risk of poverty. On a larger scale, events such as the **Great Depression** plunged huge numbers of people into joblessness and homelessness. As a direct response, governments developed relief programs in the United States and elsewhere.

Wars also can lead to poverty. A civil war in the 1990s and early 2000s in the Democratic Republic of the Congo made already high poverty rates soar. In Syria during the 2010s, people who once lived comfortably found themselves focused on just staying alive.

**STOP AND THINK:** *What other unexpected events could threaten a person or family's financial well-being?*

Natural disasters often worsen conditions for people living in poverty. For example, a person is financially struggling when a hurricane strikes the community. For weeks, there's no power,

## COVID-19 and Poverty

In recent years, progress has been made in the fight against poverty. Global rates of extreme poverty dropped from 35 percent in 1990 to 15.7 percent in 2010 to 8.2 percent in 2019. While the world wasn't fully on track to eliminate poverty by 2030, poverty rates were expected to drop to 6 percent.

But the COVID-19 pandemic reversed these gains. In 2020, 71 million people were pushed into extreme poverty, the first time rates have risen since 1998. Many businesses closed during the lockdown, leaving a large number of people out of work and unable to pay bills. Entire areas of the economy, such as travel and restaurant industries, came to a standstill. A global economic **recession** resulted, forcing people in many countries to rely on aid from government and **nonprofit** organizations. And the pandemic has hit the world's poor and **vulnerable** hardest.

Poor communities are most vulnerable to outbreaks like COVID-19.

no water, no electricity. The person can't work. With no income, the person must use savings to buy bottled water, nonperishable food, and medicine. After a storm, damaged rooftops, flooded cars, and moldy carpets all need to be fixed or replaced. But the person has to go back to work and may not have time to do the repairs. As a result, the person's health and that of their family may suffer. It may take many years to recover from the storm's financial toll.

The bottom line is that people don't *choose* to live in poverty. It doesn't result from laziness or lack of effort. It's a problem resulting from a lack of opportunity, as well as unforeseen events and outside forces.

# Related Goals

Before we move on, take a look at the full list of SDGs. Can you see how the goal of "No Poverty" overlaps with the other 16 goals? Progress on one goal often leads to progress on another. Likewise, a problem with one goal often spills over onto another. Here's an example that illustrates just how interwoven the goals are.

At Dzaleka Refugee Camp in Malawi, a woman gets a job as a seamstress making products for a **social business** called Kibébé. Before getting the job, she had no income. Her children received limited education, and the family relied on a small number of basic foods. If a family member got sick, the woman couldn't afford medicine. Now that the woman has secure work, she can send her children to school. The family can also buy a greater variety of foods and receive needed medical care.

This example shows progress not just on poverty, but also on hunger (SDG 2), health (SDG 3), education (SDG 4), and gender equity (SDG 5). Work (SDG 8), innovation (SDG 9), inequality (SDG 10), and consumption (SDG 12) are also seen in this example. Also, Kibébé often sources recycled materials to make their products, which benefits the climate (SDG 13).

This is a real example from our world. The SDGs aren't just an idea! These goals are about improving the quality of life for real people across the world, now and in the future. Now that we've started identifying problems, let's talk about *how* to solve them.

# CHAPTER 2

# Why Do We Have Goals?

Maybe it's learning to skateboard. It could be wanting to master a new language or memorize every bone in the human body. At some point, we all set goals for ourselves. But how do we get from wanting to achieve something to actually achieving it?

When organizations like the UN set goals, they use the same strategies that many people use. They break the goal down into smaller parts. Those smaller parts are often developed around the handy acronym "SMART," which stands for Specific, Measurable, Achievable, Relevant, and Timed. Say you want to learn a new language. To start, you'd make your goal more specific. You might decide that you want to watch Spanish-language movies and TV

A goal you might have is to donate more. You can start with old clothes and move on from there!

Volunteering at a soup kitchen is a great way to help the homeless in your community.

shows without subtitles. Next, you'd come up with ways to measure your progress in achieving the goal. You might aim to learn 20 new Spanish words each week by using language software at the library. To keep your goal relevant, you might keep track of new TV releases that you're eager to watch. Finally, you'd set an end date by which you would reach your goal.

**STOP AND THINK:** *What goals do you have? How could you use the SMART strategy to reach them?*

The UN's goals work exactly the same way. Goal 1 breaks down into five more specific targets:

- By 2030, end *extreme* poverty, which is living on less than $1.90 per day, per person.
- By 2030, reduce the number of men, women, and children of all ages living in poverty at least by half.
- Put national social protection systems, such as health care, in place worldwide.
- By 2030, ensure that all people, particularly the poor and vulnerable, have equal rights to economic resources and basic services.
- By 2030, build the **resilience** of the poor to reduce exposure and vulnerability to climate-related extreme events and other economic, social, and environmental shocks and disasters.

More than half a million Americans are homeless.

Each one of these targets has measurable and achievable **indicators** attached to it. A 15-year timeline is set for the whole project to be achieved. While you might think these tasks fall on governments alone, there are things that you can do to help too!

Ready to find out how you can help? Keep reading!

## What is "Universal Basic Income?"

Imagine your parents open their bank accounts to see an automatic deposit of $1,000 every month. Some leaders suggest a "universal basic income" (UBI)—or set government payments to its citizens—as a solution for poverty. Alaska has had a UBI program funded by oil revenues since 1982, which has helped wipe out extreme poverty in the state. **Advocates** say that a UBI could lead to better health, more education opportunities, and higher levels of happiness, all while reducing crime. Critics say that UBI might cost too much and make people less likely to work. What do you think? Should all people get monthly or yearly payments from the government? Do you think this is a good solution to address poverty?

# Do the Work! Contribute to the Goals at Home

**A**hh, chocolate! This superfood tastes great mixed with warm milk or blended into frozen ice cream. But did you know that cocoa fields are at the frontline of the fight against extreme poverty? Consider that there are about 5 to 6 million cocoa farmers in the world. Of those farmers, an estimated *90 percent* live in poverty. The industry also employs many child laborers, with an estimated 2 million school-age children working on cocoa plantations. Forty percent of those kids don't have the opportunity to go to school.

---

**STOP AND THINK:** *Did you know that cacao plants, which produce cocoa, grow only in a very limited tropical zone? Sixty percent of the world's chocolate is grown in the West African countries of Ghana and the Ivory Coast. Reports show that farmers in these two countries earn about 78 cents per day, well below the international extreme poverty line of $1.90.*

---

Cocoa beans are harvested from fruit called cacao.

Support local businesses that source their
materials from other local suppliers.

The choices that you and your family make about things like what chocolate you eat or what clothing you buy directly impacts people around the world. What can you do to make sure that the products you purchase have a positive rather than negative effect on people?

- **Buy Smart** — Research *what* your family buys, where it comes from, and who makes it. This way, you can make sure that the people who make it are paid a fair wage and work under safe conditions. To go back to the world of chocolate, many companies work with organizations that pay living wages to their farmers and ban child labor. Look for products with "Fair Trade" labels.

- **Skip the Gifts** — I know, I know . . . it's not easy! But for your next birthday or gift-giving holiday, consider giving rather than getting. Donations to organizations like Kiva, which provides **microloans** to **entrepreneurs** worldwide, and Heifer International, which supports small farmers, make a great gift for the whole human family.

- **Talk** — Talk about what you've learned about poverty with your family and friends. Challenge their ideas and beliefs about it. Ask them to join you in fighting poverty in your community and beyond it.

# CHAPTER 4

# Do the Work! Contribute to the Goals at School

There's nothing more powerful than a group of people working together to achieve a common goal! At schools all across the world, students are joining to take action on the SDGs. Talk to your classmates, teachers, and school administrators about trying some of the following ideas.

- **Fundraising** — At Springside Chestnut Hill Academy in Philadelphia, fifth- and sixth-grade students hold annual craft fairs and create books to raise money for Kiva loans. All profits are reinvested in small businesses across the globe.

School craft fairs are a fun way to be creative
and raise money for a good cause.

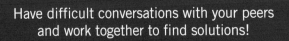

Have difficult conversations with your peers
and work together to find solutions!

- **Spark Discussion** — There's so much to learn about what people are doing to end poverty in your community and globally! Research local organizations that fight poverty in all its forms. Ask your teacher if you can invite a person from the group to speak to your class about causes of poverty and how you and your classmates can help fight it.

- **Start a Club** — It could be a book club or discussion group, but launch a club—with the help of a teacher—that examines different SDGs, teaches the school community about them, and takes action on issues. You could even examine a different SDG each month and brainstorm ways to make an impact.

---

**STOP AND THINK:** *What other types of fundraising activities could you and your classmates do? Talent shows, car washes, run-walk events . . . the opportunities are endless!*

---

# CHAPTER 5

# Do the Work! Contribute to the Goals in Your Community

"Think Global, Act Local" is a common saying of people who want to help better their communities. Learn about poverty in your town or city. Investigate its root causes. What people and groups are working to help? What can you do?

- **Host Food, Book, and Clothing Drives** — Thinking about starting a school club? That club can have a direct impact on your community! Host food, book, and clothing drives for organizations working locally or internationally. You can check out Soles4Souls for inspiration. In the process, you are acting on multiple SDGs at once, including "No Poverty," "Zero Hunger," "Quality Education," and "Climate Action."

Brainstorm ways to channel your interests to help the community.

- **Reverse Trick-or-Treat** — Wait . . . what? Trick-or-treat?! That's right! You can raise community awareness about global poverty by going door-to-door on Halloween and passing out fair trade candy. In past years, the organization Equal Exchange has worked with kids worldwide to draw attention to extreme poverty and unfair labor conditions in the cocoa industry. Equal Exchange provides trick-or-treaters with flyers and handouts to pass to candy givers.

- **Volunteer** — Community organizations always need volunteers to help in food pantries. Once you, your family, and classmates have researched groups working to end poverty in your community, reach out to see how you can help.

- **Advocate** — Write letters to your elected officials, draft petitions to politicians, and send editorials to your newspaper! Tell people about the issue and why it matters to you. Urge politicians to take action to uphold the human rights of all people to food, shelter, and housing.

**STOP AND THINK:** *Did you know that civil rights leader Martin Luther King Jr. was working on a large campaign called "The Poor People's Campaign" at the time of his death? After he was **assassinated** in April of 1968, his work for economic justice continued. On May 21, 1968, thousands of people set up a makeshift settlement on the National Mall in Washington, D.C., to draw attention to poverty. It was called Resurrection City and stood for 6 weeks. It even had its own zip code, 20013.*

# Extend Your Learning

## What Is Microfinance?

Professor Muhammad Yunus imagines a different kind of economy—one built around the idea of social business. Unlike traditional business models, social businesses consider more than profits. They also consider the effect that their business has on workers, the environment, and consumers.

The basis of social business is **microfinance**. These loans allow people all over the world to start their own businesses and move toward financial security.

Research to learn more about Muhammad Yunus, social business, and microfinance. Use the following questions to get started!

- Where and when did Yunus come up with the idea of microlending?
- Why did Yunus make his first loan?
- How was the loan helpful?
- Who benefits from microlending today? How do we know?
- Can I participate in microlending with my family or classmates? If so, how?

# Further Research

## BOOKS

Raij, Emily. *Kids Can Help Fight Poverty.* Mankato, MN: Capstone Press, 2020.

Sjonger, Rebecca. *Taking Action to End Poverty.* New York, NY: Crabtree Publishing Company, 2020.

Yoo, Paula, and Jamel Akib. *The Story of Banker of the People Muhammad Yunus.* New York, NY: Lee & Low Books, Inc., 2019.

## WEBSITES

**Goal 1: End Poverty in All Its Forms Everywhere—**
**United Nations Sustainable Development**
*www.un.org/sustainabledevelopment/poverty*
Check out the UN's Sustainable Development Goals website for more information on Goal 1.

**The Global Goals of Sustainable Development**
*margreetdeheer.com/eng/globalgoals.html*
Check out these free comics about the UN's Sustainable Development Goals.

# Glossary

**advocates** (AD-vuh-kuhts) people who support a cause or claim

**assassinated** (uh-sah-suh-NAY-tuhd) murdered for political or religious reasons

**colonial** (kuh-LOH-nee-uhl) the system or period in which one country rules another

**entrepreneurs** (ahn-truh-pruh-NUHRS) people who launch a new business

**Great Depression** (GRAYT dih-PREH-shuhn) a severe economic downturn in the late 1920s and 1930s that impacted the entire world

**indicators** (in-duh-KAY-tuhrs) measurements of progress

**microfinance** (mye-kroh-FYE-nanss) a banking system in which small loans are made to people with little or no credit history

**microloans** (mye-kroh-LOHNS) small loans to entrepreneurs and business owners, typically $100 or less

**nonprofit** (nahn-PRAH-fuht) an organization that does not seek to make a profit

**recession** (rih-SHE-shuhn) a period of economic decline

**resilience** (rih-ZIL-yuhns) the ability to recover after a disaster or catastrophe

**social business** (SOH-shuhl BIZ-nuhss) a business that puts solving social problems and helping people ahead of earning a profit

**sustainable** (suh-STAY-nuh-buhl) able to be maintained at a certain rate

**United Nations** (yuh-NYE-tuhd NAY-shuhns) the international organization that promotes peace and cooperation among nations

**vulnerable** (VUHL-nuh-ruh-buhl) susceptible to harm

**World Bank** (WURLD BANK) the international bank that provides loans and grants to low- and middle-income countries

# INDEX